7

8

Minibeasts

Christine Moorcroft

A & C BLACK • LONDON

Series consultant: Julia Stanton

Thanks to the pupils, teachers and parents from Davigdor Infant School
for taking part in the photo shoots.

A CIP record for this book is available from the British Library.

ISBN 0-7136-6218-2

First published 2003 by A & C Black Publishers Limited
37 Soho Square, London W1D 3QZ
www.acblack.com

Contents

Introduction

The Foundation Stage begins at three years old, when most children will attend some form of pre-school or nursery. These early years are critical in children's education, and the government's **Early Learning Goals** provide an indication of the skills most children should develop by the end of the Foundation Stage, which is the end of the primary school Reception year.

The Early Learning Goals cover the following areas:

- Personal, social and emotional development
- Communication, language and literacy
- Mathematical development
- Knowledge and understanding of the world
- Physical development
- Creative development

In order to achieve the Early Learning Goals, there are four levels of learning, called **Stepping Stones**. These show the knowledge, skills, understanding and attitudes that children need to develop during the Foundation Stage. Children must show progression through the Stepping Stones in order to achieve the Early Learning Goals.

The Stepping Stones have been colour coded in this pack, in line with the Foundation Stage curriculum. Yellow indicates the expected learning level at the start of the Foundation Stage and grey indicates the expected level at the end of the Foundation Stage.

- YELLOW
- BLUE
- GREEN
- GREY

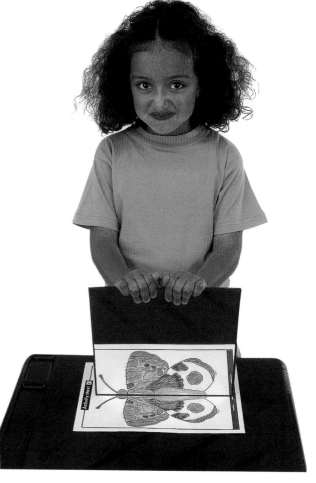

The Foundations Series

Foundations is a series of activity packs written for all adults working with children at the Foundation Stage across a range of settings: local authority nurseries; nursery centres; playgroups; pre-schools; accredited child minders in approved child minding networks; maintained schools or schools in the independent, private or voluntary sectors.

Each **Foundations** pack contains imaginative activities written specifically for those working with the Early Learning Goals and Stepping Stones. Each activity is tried and tested for suitability with children aged three to five, i.e. children at the Foundation Stage. Each book uses a popular early years theme and contains at least 40 activities that use the theme as a starting point for activities across the six key learning areas. There are also some groups of activities, such as 'Wonderful web' on pages 14-15 of this pack, which encourage children to explore one element within the theme in more detail.

Minibeasts contains all you need to plan, organise and successfully lead activities on this theme. The activities are complemented by the following resources:

- a CD of songs, poems and stories, which are integral to the activities
- a giant wall poster, which can be used for display and as a useful stimulus for many of the activities
- eight colour Photocards for use with various activities, or as stand-alone resources
- photocopiable sheets of resources, practical tasks and games to use with the activities
- ideas for displays and for developing successful links with parents and carers.

Planning and assessment

This pack provides comprehensive coverage of the Early Learning Goals and includes a planning chart to help you organise your teaching. In addition, each activity highlights which Stepping Stones are covered.

During the course of the activities, children should be assessed regularly to ensure that they develop the skills required to progress through the Stepping Stones and achieve the Early Learning Goals. The following tips will help you to plan and compile assessment records for the children.

● Keep planning and assessment records for each of the children you teach. These records can be used at the end of the Foundation Stage to produce a brief report of the child's achievements against the Early Learning Goals and Stepping Stones. The child's next teacher will find this report particularly useful if it includes the themes covered.

● Each activity covers different Stepping Stones. This allows you to choose activities that are at the correct level for the children in your group, and also provides opportunities for assessment by outcome from the activity. Use the Early Learning Goals planning chart (pages 8-9) to ensure you are covering a range of areas of learning.

● Observe what the children do and say while they are working on the activities.

● Talk to them about what they are doing. Ask questions that give the children the opportunity to give open-ended answers, and to suggest what else they might do. You can use the questions suggested with each activity for extra help.

● As part of the assessment process, keep parents and carers informed of the work their child is doing. This pack includes ideas for improving home-school links (pages 32-33) and contains suggestions for activities that can be done at home.

Handling minibeasts

Many of the activities in the book focus on collecting minibeasts from their natural habitat and examining them in a classroom setting. It is important to make it clear to the children that they must not harm the minibeasts or the environment in which they were found. You should also tell the children not to put their hands near their face or mouth after touching minibeasts and remind them to wash their hands after examining or touching them. A red symbol is shown next to every activity where you should pay special attenton to safety and hygiene.

Care must also be taken to choose appropriate containers in which to keep the minibeasts:
Insects: transparent containers, such as clear, plastic jars with air holes pierced in the lids.
Spiders: transparent containers and a damp twig. (Set spiders free immediately after the activity.)
Snails: a clear, plastic tank, such as an aquarium, containing a layer of soil and some stones (including a piece of limestone or chalk), leaves (such as lettuce) and snail food for healthy shells (ten parts oatmeal with one part calcium carbonate – available from pharmacies – mixed with water to form a paste).
Caterpillars: if possible, observe in their natural habitat, or collect for temporary observation in a large, clear container with small airholes in the lid, together with some of the plant material on which the caterpillars were found.
Worms: ice cream or margarine tubs containing damp soil.

How to use this pack

INTRODUCTION

The text in bold explains the purpose of the activity and outlines some expected outcomes.

INSTRUCTIONS

Follow the step by step instructions to find out how to prepare and carry out the activities.

Minibeast safari

RESOURCES

Transparent containers for insects and other small animals (for example, clear plastic pots with holes pierced in the lid); magnifying glasses; old spoons; paintbrushes

KNOWLEDGE AND UNDERSTANDING OF THE WORLD

Show curiosity and interest. Examine living things to find out more about them. Talk about what is seen. Investigate objects. Find out and identify some features of living things.

Key words

animal, minibeast, small

SAFETY Children will enjoy being taken outside to investigate the small animals that live in their local environment.

● Take the children for a walk around a suitable outdoor area with adult helpers.

● During the walk, point out the places in which they are likely to find minibeasts – under a stone, in cracks on a wall, in the soil, on leaves, underneath leaves, on stems and trunks and on flowers.

● Ask them to tell an adult when they have found a minibeast. Encourage them to name the minibeasts they know and help them to identify any that are difficult to recognise.

● Point out why some minibeasts cannot be collected, for example wasps and bees that may sting.

● Ask the adults to collect minibeast samples and to talk about what they are doing – for example, using a spoon to scoop up a worm with some soil and leaves, using a paintbrush to flick an ant or ladybird into a container (always put in material from its habitat).

● Discuss why the children must wash their hands when they come back indoors.

Questions

What minibeasts can you find?
Do you know what it is called?
Where did you find it?
What can you tell me about it?
Why should you wash your hands when you come inside?

What have we found?

RESOURCES

Magnifying glasses; containers; CD-ROMs and information books about insects and other small animals

PHOTOCARDS   POSTER

KNOWLEDGE AND UNDERSTANDING OF THE WORLD

Show curiosity and interest. Examine living things to find out more about them. Talk about what is seen. Investigate objects. Find out about and identify some features of living things.

Key words

ant, beetle, centipede, millipede, small, woodlouse (and any other minibeasts found)

SAFETY Back indoors, consolidate the children's understanding of minibeasts through close observation and questioning.

● Collect a number of minibeasts, making sure to gather some of their food as well.

● Show the children how to use a magnifying glass to examine the minibeasts.

● Remind them not to touch their eyes, mouths or faces after handling minibeasts, or the containers and their contents.

● Help the children to use the Poster, some of the Photocards, and other reference material to identify the animals.

● Encourage them to ask questions about the parts of the minibeasts. This will help them identify which one is which.

● Point out that photographs and drawings usually show animals much bigger than they really are. Help the children to understand scale by drawing their attention to the size of the leaves or flowers on the Photocards.

Questions

Does it have legs?
Can you count the legs?
Does it have wings? How many?
How does it move?
What colour is it?
Is it long or short?
What else can you see?

Extension

Ask the children to draw a picture of one of the minibeasts they found. Encourage them to tell you something about their minibeast.

11

EARLY LEARNING GOALS

This heading indicates the main Early Learning Goal upon which the activity focuses. (See pages 8-9 for other Early Learning Goals that are also covered.)

STEPPING STONES

These are key skills which the activity develops. The colour of the text indicates the corresponding Stepping Stone level in the Foundation Stage curriculum (see page 4).

RESOURCES

This box lists the resources you will need for each activity.

Resources included in the pack are represented by an icon. These could be one of the following:
● Poster
● Activity Sheet
● Photocard
● CD

KEY WORDS

This box contains key vocabulary that the children will encounter in the course of the activity.

QUESTIONS

Each activity has a prompt box of questions you could ask the children during the activity.

EXTENSION

Some activities feature a further activity that extends and consolidates the children's understanding of the main activity.

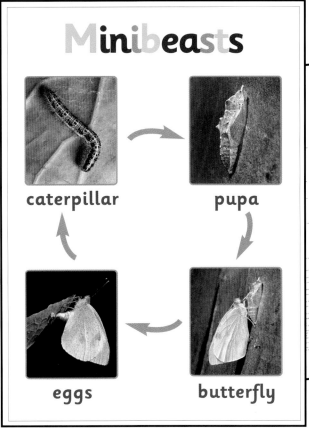

Wall poster

This giant poster can be used to introduce the topic of Minibeasts and also provides a useful centrepiece for a display. The words to the songs and poems on the CD are printed on the back of the poster and are accompanied by illustrations. Before putting up the poster, you may wish to enlarge the text on a photocopier for some of the children to follow as they listen to the CD. This will help the children begin to recognise words, even if they cannot 'read' the whole text. The words and illustrations can also be used as part of your display. You may wish to Tippex out the track numbers before photocopying the pages.

Photocards

The Photocards can often be used to start an activity and have been chosen to prompt discussion. The questions box offers suggestions of what to ask the children while you are using the Photocards. Try to work with a small group of children so that each picture can be seen clearly. You may also wish to start a collection, adding further photographs and magazine pictures from other sources.

Activity Sheets

Photocopiable Activity Sheets are provided to support particular activities. In some cases, a sheet may be used with a small group, whilst for other activities each child will need their own copy. The Activity Sheets can be enlarged to A3, copied onto card and laminated so that they last longer. You might also wish to colour in the games.

CD

This CD will play on a CD player or computer with a CD drive and sound facility. Alternatively, you can copy the CD onto an audiotape if you do not have access to a CD player in your setting. The CD includes songs, rhymes, poems and music – all of which are integrated into various activities. Each track is indicated by a numbered CD icon in the resources box. Transcripts of all CD tracks appear on the back of the Minibeasts poster.

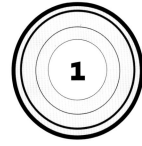

Planning chart

The planning chart below is to help you to plan your coverage of the Early Learning Goals and to enable you to match the activities to the children's ability levels, indicated by the Stepping Stones. Each activity focuses on one main Early Learning Goal (indicated by a black circle in the planning chart) and may also cover secondary Early Learning Goals (indicated by a blank circle). There are two ways in which you may wish to use this chart:

- **Start with the Early Learning Goals and Stepping Stones**
  Decide which main Early Learning Goal you would like to cover and at what level (i.e. Stepping Stone). Use the planning chart below to choose an activity that meets your requirements. Refer to the activity page for a more detailed outline of the Stepping Stones covered by the activity. Ensure you keep a record of the Early Learning Goals and Stepping Stones you cover.

- **Start with the activities**
  From the chart below, choose an activity that is appropriate for your setting. Keep a record of the Early Learning Goals and Stepping Stones covered by the activity.

Early Learning Goals → / Stepping Stones →	Personal, social and emotional development				Communication, language and literacy				Mathematical development				Knowledge and understanding of the world				Physical development				Creative development			
	YELLOW	BLUE	GREEN	GREY	YELLOW	BLUE	GREEN	GREY	YELLOW	BLUE	GREEN	GREY	YELLOW	BLUE	GREEN	GREY	YELLOW	BLUE	GREEN	GREY	YELLOW	BLUE	GREEN	GREY
Will it fit? (p10)	○	○	○	○					●	●	●	●												
What is a minibeast? (p10)					●	●	●	●					○	○	○	○								
Minibeast safari (p11)	○	○	○	○	○	○	○	○					●	●	●	●								
What have we found? (p11)	○	○	○	○	○	○	○	○	○	○	○	○	●	●	●	●								
Guess who? (p12)					●	●	●	●					○	○	○	○								
The ants go marching (p12)									●	●	●	●					○	○	○	○	○	○	○	○
Be a minibeast (p13)					●	●	●	●									○	○	○	○	○	○	○	○
Where do I live? (p13)					●	●	●	●					○	○	○	○								
WONDERFUL WEB																								
What is a web? (p14)					○	○	○	○					●	●	●	●								
Bingo web (p14)					●	●	●	●					○	○	○	○								
Frosted web patterns (p15)													○	○	○	○					●	●	●	●
Under a web (p15)									●	●	●	●									○	○	○	○
Little Miss Muffet (p16)					●	●	●	●																

Early Learning Goals →	Personal, social and emotional development	Communication, language and literacy	Mathematical development	Knowledge and understanding of the world	Physical development	Creative development
Spider places (p16)	● ● ● ●	○ ○ ○ ○				
Shoo fly (p17)		● ● ● ●				
Dragonfly (p17)		○ ○ ○ ○				● ● ● ●
Snailwatch (p18)	○ ○ ○ ○	○ ○ ○ ○		● ● ● ●		
Snail's lunch (p18)		● ● ● ●		○ ○ ○ ○		
Spirals (p19)		○ ○ ○ ○				● ● ● ●
Snail trail (p19)		○ ○ ○ ○				● ● ● ●
CATERPILLAR LIFE STORY						
Crawling caterpillar (p20)		○ ○ ○ ○		● ● ● ●		○ ○ ○ ○
Inside a cocoon (p20)				● ● ●		
Laying eggs (p21)		○ ○ ○ ○		● ● ● ●		
Beautiful butterfly (p21)		○ ○ ○ ○	○ ○ ○ ○			● ● ● ●
WORMS						
Wormwatch (p22)	○ ○ ○ ○			● ● ● ●		
Long worm, short worm? (p22)			● ● ● ●	○ ○ ○ ○		
Squirmy earthworm (p23)		● ● ● ●				○ ○ ○ ○
Magic growing pictures (p23)			○ ○ ○ ○		● ● ● ●	
Look — no legs! (p24)					● ● ● ●	
What do mini-beasts eat? (p24)		○ ○ ○ ○		● ● ● ●		
Ladybird, ladybird (p25)		● ● ● ●				
Ladybird spots (p25)			● ● ● ●	○ ○ ○ ○		
A taste of honey (p26)	● ● ● ●	○ ○ ○ ○				
Honeycomb print (p26)	○ ○ ○ ○	○ ○ ○ ○	○ ○ ○ ○			● ● ● ●
Buzzing bees (p27)				○ ○ ○ ○		● ● ● ●
William the worm (p27)		● ● ● ●				
MINIBEAST MENAGERIE						
Minibeast homes (p28)				● ● ● ●		
Create a zoo (p28)	● ● ● ●	○ ○ ○ ○				○ ○ ○ ○
Going to the zoo (p29)	○ ○ ○ ○	○ ○ ○ ○				● ● ● ●
Minibeasts big book (p29)		● ● ● ●		○ ○ ○ ○		

Will it fit?

RESOURCES

Per group of three, matchbox, everyday objects (some of which will fit into a matchbox and some that will not)

Activity Sheet 1

MATHEMATICAL DEVELOPMENT

Show an interest in shape and space. Use shapes appropriately for tasks. Compare two items by length or height. Use language such as 'greater' and 'smaller'.

Key words

bigger, fit, same, small, smaller, tiny

This prediction activity will help to develop the children's understanding of size and will improve their vocabulary.

- Photocopy Activity Sheet 1 – one per group of three children.

- Show the children a matchbox. Point to a very large object – a table or cupboard – and ask the children if it would fit into the matchbox. Repeat for other objects.

- Give each group a collection of objects and a matchbox. Ask them to predict which objects will fit into the matchbox.

- With each group, discuss which object 'fits' or 'does not fit'. Ask the children to name them.

- Hand out a copy of Activity Sheet 1 to each group. Encourage the children to identify each animal and to predict whether it will fit into their matchbox.

- Help them to cut out the animals and see if they will fit into the matchbox.

Questions

Will the cupboard/table fit into the matchbox?
Is it bigger or smaller than the matchbox?
Is it the same size as the matchbox?
Which of these objects will fit into the matchbox?

Extension

Give each group a piece of paper folded into a 'book'. Ask the children to paste each minibeast onto a page. Provide them with labels for their minibeasts and see if they can find the correct label to put onto each page.

What is a minibeast?

RESOURCES

Car brochures showing pictures of a Mini

COMMUNICATION, LANGUAGE AND LITERACY

Use action with limited talk. Use talk to give new meaning to objects. Begin to make patterns in experience through sequencing, ordering and grouping. Extend vocabulary, especially by grouping or naming. Use talk to organise, sequence and clarify thinking.

Key words

animal, mini, minibeast, small, tiny, very

This activity introduces the term 'minibeasts' and further develops the children's understanding of size.

- Ask the children if they have heard the word 'mini' before. Have they seen a minibus or a Mini car? Show them pictures of the car and tell them it is called a Mini because it is smaller than other cars.

- Invite the children to make up some 'mini' words for very small versions of house, teddy, doll, chair, pencil and dog. What other 'mini' words can they make up?

- If the children have not thought of it already, introduce the term 'minibeast', and explain that it is a creature that is so small it will usually fit into a matchbox.

- Encourage the children to give you all the names of creatures they think are minibeasts. Write them on the whiteboard and discuss which are actually minibeasts.

Questions

Do you know what 'mini' means?
Have you ever been in a minibus?
How is it different from a normal bus?
Do you know what a Mini car is?
Is it a big or small car?
Do you know what a miniskirt is?
Which animals are minibeasts?

Minibeast safari

SAFETY **Children will enjoy being taken outside to investigate the small animals that live in their local environment.**

RESOURCES

Transparent containers for insects and other small animals (for example, clear plastic pots with holes pierced in the lid); magnifying glasses; old spoons; paintbrushes

KNOWLEDGE AND UNDERSTANDING OF THE WORLD

Show curiosity and interest. Examine living things to find out more about them. Talk about what is seen. Investigate objects. Find out and identify some features of living things.

Key words

animal, minibeast, small

● Take the children for a walk around a suitable outdoor area with adult helpers.

● During the walk, point out the places in which they are likely to find minibeasts – under a stone, in cracks on a wall, in the soil, on leaves, underneath leaves, on stems and trunks and on flowers.

● Ask them to tell an adult when they have found a minibeast. Encourage them to name the minibeasts they know and help them to identify any that are difficult to recognise.

● Point out why some minibeasts cannot be collected, for example wasps and bees that may sting.

● Ask the adults to collect minibeast samples and to talk about what they are doing – for example, using a spoon to scoop up a worm with some soil and leaves, using a paintbrush to flick an ant or ladybird into a container (always put in material from its habitat).

● Discuss why the children must wash their hands when they come back indoors.

Questions

What minibeasts can you find?
Do you know what it is called?
Where did you find it?
What can you tell me about it?
Why should you wash your hands when you come inside?

What have we found?

RESOURCES

Magnifying glasses; containers; CD-ROMs and information books about insects and other small animals

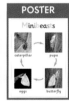

KNOWLEDGE AND UNDERSTANDING OF THE WORLD

Show curiosity and interest. Examine living things to find out more about them. Talk about what is seen. Investigate objects. Find out about and identify some features of living things.

Key words

ant, beetle, centipede, millipede, small, woodlouse (and any other minibeasts found)

SAFETY **Back indoors, consolidate the children's understanding of minibeasts through close observation and questioning.**

● Collect a number of minibeasts, making sure to gather some of their food as well.

● Show the children how to use a magnifying glass to examine the minibeasts.

● Remind them not to touch their eyes, mouths or faces after handling minibeasts, or the containers and their contents.

● Help the children to use the Poster, some of the Photocards, and other reference material to identify the animals.

● Encourage them to ask questions about the parts of the minibeasts. This will help them identify which one is which.

● Point out that photographs and drawings usually show animals much bigger than they really are. Help the children to understand scale by drawing their attention to the size of the leaves or flowers on the Photocards.

Questions

Does it have legs?
Can you count the legs?
Does it have wings? How many?
How does it move?
What colour is it?
Is it long or short?
What else can you see?

Extension

Ask the children to draw a picture of one of the minibeasts they found. Encourage them to tell you something about their minibeast.

Guess who?

I am a worm
I have 0 legs

I am a bee
I have 6 legs

I am a snail
I have 0 legs

I am an ant
I have 6 legs

RESOURCES

Pencils

**COMMUNICATION,
LANGUAGE AND LITERACY**

Use vocabulary focused on objects of importance. Build up vocabulary that reflects the breadth of experience. Extend vocabulary by naming things. Extend vocabulary explaining the meanings of new words.

Key words

minibeast, animal, snail, worm, bee, ant, wings, legs, how many? numbers from one to six

Encourage the children to ask questions and develop their observational skills as they play this guessing game.

● Photocopy Activity Sheet 2 – one per child – and hand them out.

● Choose a minibeast from the Activity Sheet. The children have to guess which minibeast you have selected by asking questions such as 'Does it have legs?' and 'Can it fly?'.

● Once the children have guessed the minibeast correctly, help them to label it by writing over the dots on their sheet.

● Invite a child to choose another minibeast for the class to guess.

● Now, divide the children into pairs and ask them to continue the game. The game is over when all of the blanks on their sheets are filled in.

Questions

Does the minibeast have wings?
Can it fly?
Does it have legs?
Does it move fast or slowly?
Is it long or short?

Extension

Allow the children to cut out the pictures on the Activity Sheet and make a freize or play snap with them.

The ants go marching

RESOURCES

MATHEMATICAL DEVELOPMENT

Show an interest in numbers and counting. Use number names. Enjoy joining in number rhymes. Recognise one, two or three objects. Count up to six objects. Say and use number names in order in familiar contexts.

Key words

march, number words from one to ten

This song will help to develop the children's interest in numbers and counting, and they will also enjoy singing along and responding to the rhythm.

● Play the song 'The ants go marching', and make up some actions for the children to copy.

● The children could march to the song by walking single file for 'one by one', in pairs for 'two by two' and so on.

● Once they can carry out the marching actions, you could introduce the action for the second line of each verse – 'the little one stopped to do up his shoe', and so on.

Questions

How many ants are marching?
Can you shown me three ants marching?
Can you march one by one?
Can you march two by two?

Extension

Using sponges, encourage the children to print the bodies of the ants marching one by one, two by two and so on. Ask them to add the legs using a pencil or brush and paint.

Be a minibeast

RESOURCES

COMMUNICATION, LANGUAGE AND LITERACY

Use words and gestures to communicate. Listen to songs and join in repeated refrains. Respond to simple instructions. Build up vocabulary that reflects experiences. Extend vocabulary. Extend vocabulary exploring the meaning of new words.

Key words

crawl, dart, flutter, fly, jump, scuttle, slide, wriggle, zoom

This activity will develop the children's coordination and vocabulary, as they mime and describe how minibeasts move.

- Play the 'Be a minibeast' song.

- Ask the children how they would 'be a worm' – talk about how it moves along the ground, and ask them to repeat the word 'wriggle'. Demonstrate the action.

- Ask the children how they would 'be a spider' – talk about how it moves, and ask them to repeat the word 'scuttle'.

- Play the song again and encourage the children to mime the actions and join in with the words.

- With the children, make up a verse about another minibeast, for instance a butterfly. Talk about how it moves through the air. Sing their verse with them to the music on the CD. Repeat this for other minibeasts the children have observed.

Questions

How does a worm/caterpillar/snail move?
Which minibeast slithers?
Which minibeast steps?
Which minibeast stretches?
Can you think of a minibeast that flies/walks?

Extension

Choose one of the children to be a minibeast 'statue'. Ask the others which minibeast they think the child is. Can anyone make a different shape for that minibeast?

Where do I live?

RESOURCES

COMMUNICATION, LANGUAGE AND LITERACY

Respond to simple instructions. Listen to stories with increasing attention and recall. Extend vocabulary by grouping or naming. Sustain attentive listening, responding by relevant comments, questions or actions.

Key words

flower, leaf, soil, stem, stone, trunk, twig, in, under, on top of, web, behind

Use this activity to develop the children's listening skills as they examine minibeast environments in more detail.

- Photocopy Activity Sheet 3 – one per pair.

- During circle time, discuss minibeast habitats with the children.

- Play the listening skills track 'Where does it live?' and encourage the children to pay close attention as they listen.

- Show the children Photocard 1 and play the track again. Pause after each description and ask the children to guess which minibeast is being described, and where on the photocard it might live.

- Explain that some minibeasts may live in more than one place.

- Ask the children to choose a partner and hand out the Activity Sheet. Encourage them to name the minibeasts on the sheet.

- Ask each pair to decide which minibeast belongs in which habitat on the Activity Sheet. Play the track a final time and ask the children to draw a line from each minibeast to the habitat in which it belongs.

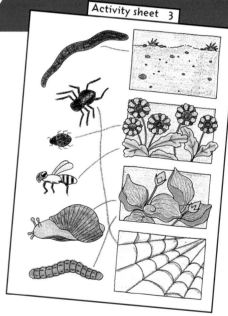

Questions

Which minibeast is being described?
How do you know?
Where does it belong on the picture?

Extension

If you have made a large minibeast display picture (see pages 30-31), help the children to cut out their Activity Sheet minibeasts and place them in the correct place.

WONDERFUL WEB

This group of activities will inspire the children's sense of curiosity and wonder about webs and spiders.

What is a web?

RESOURCES

If possible, some real spiders — kept for the duration of the activity only (see p5)

PHOTOCARD 2

KNOWLEDGE AND UNDERSTANDING OF THE WORLD

Show an interest in why things happen. Talk about what is seen. Examine objects to find out more about them. Investigate objects using all senses as appropriate.

Key words

catch, flies, spider, stick, trap, web

● Show the children Photocard 2 and ask them what it shows.

● Write the word 'web' on the whiteboard and invite the children to repeat it. Ask them to think of other words that begin with 'w'. Write these words on the whiteboard.

● Encourage the children to talk about the pattern and colour of the web, and to discuss why they think it is white.

● Ask the children what made the web. Point out the spider in the middle of the web and ask if they know how the web helps the spider.

● Talk about how the spider spins sticky threads for its web, to trap flies and other minibeasts for its food.

● Finish by listening to the short poem 'What a sad sight', and encourage the children to discuss it in a small group.

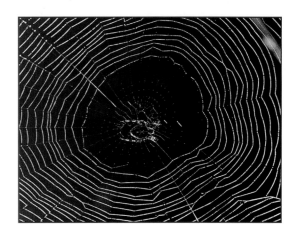

Questions

Do you know what made the web?
What has made the web white?
Why do you think a minibeast would be in the web?
How does the picture make you feel? Why?
Would you feel sad at seeing flies caught in a web?

Bingo web

RESOURCES

Small counters

Activity Sheet 4

COMMUNICATION, LANGUAGE AND LITERACY

Distinguish one sound from another. Understand the concept of a word. Hear and say the initial sound in words and know which letters represent some of the sounds. Link sounds to letters.

Key words

web, wall, well, wheel, worm

● Photocopy Activity Sheet 4 – one per pair of children, and one for yourself.

● Cut out the eighteen bingo squares on your copy and put them in a hat so you can draw them out one at a time. Cut out the children's bingo cards from the Activity Sheets.

● Ask the children to choose a partner and give each pair two different bingo cards and some counters. Make sure the children can identify all of the minibeasts on the cards and ask them which ones the spider would most like to find in its web.

● Explain to the children that when you draw a minibeast out of the hat and call out its name, they should find that minibeast on their card and put a counter over it.

● When three minibeasts in a row are covered, they can call 'Spider Bingo!'. The game is over when you have drawn all of the squares out of the hat. Play another game.

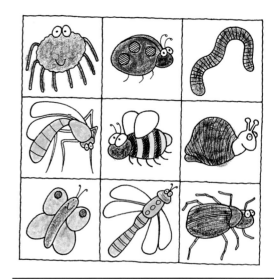

Questions

What does a spider like to eat?
Which minibeasts would you find in a spider's web?
What is the first letter of the word 'web'?

Frosted web patterns

RESURCES

Per child, 1 piece of stiff, black paper, white chalk

CREATIVE DEVELOPMENT

Explore texture and space. Differentiate marks and movements on paper. Understand that different media can be combined. Explore colour, texture, shape, form and space in two dimensions.

Key words

black, chalk, line, straight, white

● Encourage the children to look carefully at Photocard 2.

● Invite them to study and describe the lines on the web in detail.

● Demonstrate how to draw on black paper with chalk, then ask the children to draw their own webs.

● Display the children's drawings next to Photocard 2 and encourage them to look for similarities and differences.

● Invite the children to talk about any changes they could make to their drawings, such as making the webs bigger.

Questions

Are the lines on the web straight?
What colour are the lines?
How is your web different from the picture on the Photocard?

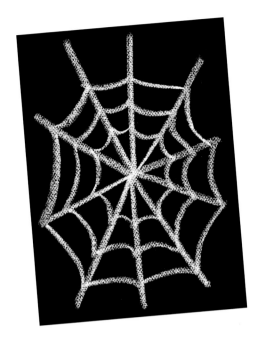

Under a web

RESOURCES

MATHEMATICAL DEVELOPMENT

Enjoy joining in number rhymes and songs. Compare two groups of objects, saying when they have the same number, more or fewer. Show curiosity about numbers. Recognise numbers. Count up to eight objects. Say and use number names in familiar contexts. Count reliably up to 10 objects.

Key words

any, bee, cat, spider, worm, none, two, four, six, eight,

● Before the activity, photocopy Activity Sheet 5 – one per child.

● Play the song 'Under a web', encouraging the children to listen carefully. Next, ask the children to name the animals in the song, and to say how many legs each one has.

● Show them '0' for 'none'. Ask them to name a minibeast that has no legs.

● Play the song again and make up some actions for the spider, bee, cat and worm.

● Hand out Activity Sheet 5 to each child. Talk about each picture, and ask them to count the number of legs on each minibeast.

● Explain that they are going to match each minibeast to a number which shows how many legs it has. Show them how to draw a line from each minibeast to the correct number.

Questions

What animals are in the song?
How many legs do they have?
Can you write the number 0/2/4/6/8?

Activity sheet 5

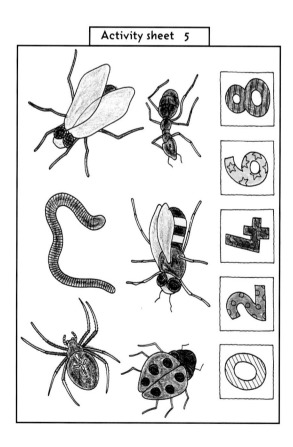

Extension

Help the children to make a class bar graph showing the number of minibeasts they have seen over a week (x axis) and the number of legs they have (y axis).

Little Miss Muffet

RESOURCES

Scissors; glue; paper

COMMUNICATION, LANGUAGE AND LITERACY

Listen to favourite nursery rhymes. Enjoy rhyming and rhythmic activities. Show awareness of rhyme. Begin to recognise some familiar words. Listen with enjoyment and respond to stories and songs, rhymes and poems and make up own songs, rhymes and poems.

Key words

rhyme, spider

Recite this well-known nursery rhyme with the children and then encourage them to sort out the pictures so that the story is in the correct order.

● Photocopy Activity Sheet 6 – one per child.

● Play the 'Little Miss Muffet' song. Repeat the song, stopping at intervals and asking the children what comes next.

● Draw the children's attention to the rhyme 'muffet' and 'tuffet'.

● Now hand out the Activity Sheet. Explain that the 'Little Miss Muffet' pictures are mixed up. Show them how to cut out the pictures.

● Ask four children to come to the front of the class with different pictures. Invite them to put themselves and the pictures in the correct order as you replay the nursery rhyme.

● Play the 'Little Miss Muffet' song again and ask the children to join in and follow the story. At the end they can stick their own pictures onto a piece of paper in the correct order.

Questions

What is the song about?
What is Little Miss Muffet doing?
What words come next?
What is a tuffet?
Can you put the words and pictures in the right order?

Extension

Ask the children to suggest other rhymes. Give them examples such as 'Little Miss Blair, She sat on a … (chair)', 'Little Tom Poor, He sat on the … (floor)'.

Spider places

RESOURCES

PERSONAL, SOCIAL AND EMOTIONAL DEVELOPMENT

Seek out others to share experiences. Show confidence in linking up with others for guidance and support. Display high levels of involvement in activities. Have a developing awareness of own needs, news and feelings and be sensitive to those of others.

Key words

afraid, frightened, scared, spider

The song 'Incy Wincy Spider' is a good starting point to help the children understand why some people are afraid of spiders.

● Photocopy Activity Sheet 7 – one per child.

● Remind the children of the nursery rhyme 'Little Miss Muffet'. Explain that she might not have been frightened of spiders, but was suddenly surprised to see such a big spider.

● Play the 'Incy Wincy Spider' song.

● Hand out Activity Sheet 7. Ask the children if they can find the spider.

● With a small group, discuss the other frames on the Activity Sheet, such as the attic and the bicycle frame. Encourage the children to discuss whether they think they would find spiders in any of these habitats. Ask them if they would be afraid if they found a spider in one of these places.

● Ask the children to draw webs onto the Activity Sheet where they would expect to find them.

● Talk about what they can do to feel less scared of spiders (and other minibeasts). For example, they could look at pictures in books.

Questions

How did Little Miss Muffet feel about spiders?
Did the spider make her jump?
Are you afraid of spiders? Why?
What are you afraid of?
What other things are people afraid of?

Extension

Ask the children to colour in the pictures on the Activity Sheet. Encourage them to draw a spider web and spider in each habitat.

Shoo fly

RESOURCES

Per pair, large cube; dark coloured crayons

COMMUNICATION, LANGUAGE AND LITERACY

Use familiar words. Build up vocabulary that reflects experiences. Extend vocabulary. Extend vocabulary exploring the meanings of new words.

Key words

body, feeler, head, leg, wing, fly

The children will enjoy this fly game and it will also develop their vocabulary for the different parts of an insect's body.

● Photocopy Activity Sheet 8 – three copies per pair. Make a die per pair by cutting out the fly body parts from one sheet and gluing them to the sides of a large cube.

● Introduce the word 'fly' and talk about the children's experience of flies – where they have seen them, what they look like, what they eat and what they do.

● Explain how to play the game. In pairs, the children take turns to roll the die and colour the part of the fly shown on their sheet, until they have coloured the entire fly. If they roll the same part twice, they miss their turn and pass the die to their partner.

● Encourage the children to say the names of the body parts shown on the die each time they roll it.

● Finish by playing 'There was an old lady who swallowed a fly'.

Questions

How many bodies/heads/feelers/legs does a fly have?
What do you need to finish your fly?
What is the name of this part?

Dragonfly

RESOURCES

Tissue paper; clear coloured acetate or cellophane; glitter; cardboard tubes; card; shiny thread; pipe cleaners

CREATIVE DEVELOPMENT

Explore texture and space. Begin to describe the texture of things. Experiment to create different textures. Choose colours to use for a purpose. Explore colour, texture, shape, form and space in two or three dimensions.

Key words

bright, clear, long, see-through, shiny, sparkling, thick, thin

This model-making activity will develop the children's appreciation of shape, colour and texture.

● Show the children Photocard 3. Invite them to guess what it shows.

● Ask them about parts of the dragonfly, such as its head, body and wings. Point out the animal's large size for an insect (approx 3cm).

● Explain to the children that they are going to help you make a model of a dragonfly.

● Talk about the colours and textures of the materials they can use.

● Start by covering a cardboard tube with tissue paper, then attach wings made from acetate or cellophane, legs made from pipe cleaners and eyes from cardboard.

● Finish by listening to the poem 'A Dragonfly'. Ask the children to listen carefully to find out what the dragonfly did and what it looked like.

Questions

What is special about the size of the dragonfly's wings?
Are the dragonfly's wings thick or thin/shiny or dull?
Which parts look light and delicate/solid and thick?

Extension

Invite the children to use one hand to imitate the action of a dragonfly landing on their other hand. Encourage them to think about how it will land. Demonstrate a crash landing and a gentle, light landing.

Snailwatch

RESOURCES

Snail; magnifying glasses; piece of perspex about 20cm x 12cm, a clear container (see guidelines for keeping snails on page 5)

PHOTOCARD 4

KNOWLEDGE AND UNDERSTANDING OF THE WORLD

Show curiosity. Describe simple features of objects. Examine living things to find out more about them. Find out about, and identify, some features of living things.

Key words
body, feelers, mouth, shell, slime, snail, squeeze, stretch

SAFETY **Allow the children to examine real snails. As they do so, discuss their observations and encourage them to take care of living things.**

● Show a small group of children Photocard 4 and invite them to guess what the animal is. Discuss any similarities with other animals, for example it has no legs – like a worm.

● Tell the group that they are going to look at a real snail, and that they must keep their snail safe. Explain that they must handle it gently. Reassure them that they need not touch it if they do not want to.

● Place a snail on a piece of perspex or in a clear container and show each child, in turn, how to examine the snail by using a magnifying glass.

● Invite them to talk about what they see. Hold up the perspex and encourage the children to observe the snail from underneath.

● Help them to describe how the snail moves by using words such as 'squeeze' and 'stretch'.

● Return the snail to its habitat, and tell the children that it is not kind to keep snails away from their habitat for too long.

Questions
Can you find the snail's mouth?
Does it have eyes?
What is the snail doing?
How does it move?
Do you know what a snail leaves behind?

Snail's lunch

RESOURCES

Crayons

PHOTOCARD 4 — Activity Sheet 9

10

COMMUNICATION, LANGUAGE AND LITERACY

Use words and gestures to communicate. Build up vocabulary that reflects the breadth of experiences. Extend vocabulary by grouping and naming. Extend vocabulary, explain meanings of new words.

Key words
body, feelers, head, mouth, shell, slime, snail

What are the different parts of the snail called and what do snails like to eat? Children can find out with the help of a poem, photograph and Activity Sheet.

● Photocopy Activity Sheet 9 – one per child.

● Begin by playing the poem 'Snail'. Discuss what the poem says about snails.

Activity sheet 9

● Show the children Photocard 4 and invite them to point to the body parts as you say them: body, feelers, head, mouth, shell. Encourage them to say the words. Write them onto the whiteboard for the children to see.

● Give each child a copy of Activity Sheet 9. Ask the children to suggest which of the foods on the sheet they think the snail would like to eat.

● Encourage them to draw a line from the snail to the food they like to eat.

Questions
Can you see the snail's body/eyes?
Does it have legs/arms/wings?
What shape is the shell?
How many feelers does it have?
Which part of the snail is soft/hard?

Extension
Put the Photocard on the board. Ask the children to take turns drawing a line from the Photocard to labels for the snail parts.

Spirals

RESOURCES

Per group, snail, piece of perspex about 20 cm x 12 cm; paper; wax crayons or paint; brushes

CREATIVE DEVELOPMENT

Show an interest in what they see, hear, touch and feel. Try to capture experiences with paint and other materials. Differentiate marks and movements on paper. Work creatively on a large or small scale. Explore colour, texture and shape, form and space in two or three dimensions.

Key words

curly, round, shell, snail, spiral, middle, inside, outside

Encourage the children to experiment with spiral patterns, using the snails they have examined as their inspiration.

● Give a group of children a snail on a piece of perspex.

● Ask the children to look at the shape and pattern of the snail's shell.

● Help them to describe it using the words 'round' and 'curly'.

● Introduce the word 'spiral', and demonstrate a spiral by drawing it in the air, inviting them to do the same.

● Provide paper and wax crayons or brushes and paint and ask the children to draw some spirals in different colours.

● Ask them if they started in the middle or on the outside of the spiral, and encourage them to try both. Ask the children which way makes the better spiral?

● Demonstrate clockwise and anti-clockwise spirals and encourage the children to try both.

Questions

Can you see something round/curly?
Can you draw a curly thing?
What curly things do you know?
Can you draw a spiral in the air with your finger?

Extension

Encourage the children to look for other spirals in the environment and in non-fiction books – for example, a spiral staircase, a pattern on fabric, wallpaper, a circular raffia mat or the bottom of a basket.

Snail trail

RESOURCES

A large bowl (for example a washing-up bowl); small bowls and bottles; spoons; plastic sieves; play 'slime' made from: 500g cornflour 300ml water (food dye added until the desired colour is achieved)

CREATIVE DEVELOPMENT

Use their bodies to explore texture and space. Begin to describe the texture of things. Further explore an experience using a range of senses. Work creatively on a large or small scale. Explore colour, texture, shape, form and space in two or three dimensions.

Key words

slime, slimy, slippery, sloppy, squeeze, wet, green, yellow

Children will love playing with slime! As they do so, help them to talk about how it feels.

● Provide a bowl full of 'play slime' and encourage small groups of children to explore its texture by picking it up in their hands, trying to pour it and squeeze it.

● Introduce equipment with which to manipulate it, for example spoons, cups, small bowls and plastic bottles.

● Encourage the children to talk about what they are doing and what they find out.

● Introduce words to describe the slime and words for its colour. Explain to the children that slime helps a snail move.

Questions

Can you make shapes with the slime?
Can you pour it into a bottle?
What happens when you take a big handful of slime?
How does the slime feel?
Does the slime go through a sieve?

Extension

Encourage the children to experiment to see if different classroom objects, such as a pencil, move more or less easily on the slime.

CATERPILLAR LIFE STORY

Use this group of activities to help the children understand the life cycle of a caterpillar – how it becomes a pupa and then a butterfly or moth.

Crawling caterpillar

● If possible, take the children outside to look for caterpillars or show them Photocard 5. Encourage them to look closely and to describe the caterpillar.

● Let the children watch (not touch) the caterpillars. Then ask them to demonstrate, using their hands, how the caterpillars move.

● Suggest words that describe how the caterpillar moves – arch, hump, legs, stretch.

● Play the song 'Caterpillars only crawl'. Encourage the children to move their hands to the music, imitating the movement of a caterpillar along their arm.

Extension

The children could try moving like caterpillars, first stretching their bodies, making them as long as they can and then arching them into a hump. Encourage them to say 'stretch' slowly as they stretch and to say 'arch' as they form an arch.

Inside a cocoon

● Play 'The caterpillar' poem while the children listen.

● Talk about what the poem tells us about the caterpillar – where it is seen, what it is doing on the leaf and what happens to it.

● Ask the children to look at the caterpillar on the Poster. Discuss why it would spend a lot of time on a leaf.

● Now ask them to look at the pictures of the pupa and the butterfly. Explain that the caterpillar forms a skin around itself, (called a cocoon), and becomes a pupa. Tell the children that inside, the caterpillar is turning into a butterfly, which comes out of the cocoon after staying inside it, sometimes for many days.

● Ask the children to draw pictures to illustrate these stages in the life story of a caterpillar. Display the pictures in order in a straight line. Help them to 'write' captions for their pictures.

← Pupa

Laying eggs

RESOURCES

Books about butterflies; paper; crayons

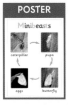

13

KNOWLEDGE AND UNDERSTANDING OF THE WORLD

Show curiosity. Describe simple features of objects. Examine living things to find out more about them. Find out and identify some features of living things.

Key words

body, butterfly, caterpillar, cocoon, egg, feelers, head, lay, moth, pupa, wings

● Begin by playing the track 'Tiny caterpillar', asking the children to join in with the words.

● Ask the children how the caterpillar got on to the leaf and where it came from.

● Show them the Poster or an information book about butterflies, explaining that the butterfly lays eggs on leaves so that when the baby caterpillars hatch, they will find food.

● Help the children to retell the story of the caterpillar. Ask them to draw new pictures to add to the beginning of their display: one showing a butterfly laying its eggs on a leaf and one of the eggs hatching into caterpillars.

● Add the new pictures to the display of the caterpillar's life story. Ask the children where they are going to put the part about the butterfly laying eggs.

● Reread the story with the children.

Questions

Where did the caterpillar come from?
Where did the egg come from?
Where did the butterfly come from?
Where did the pupa come from?
How do you know?

Extension

Read 'The Very Hungry Caterpillar' by Eric Carle with the children.

Beautiful butterfly

RESOURCES

Per group, plastic mirror; book about butterflies; crayons

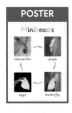

Activity Sheet

10

14

CREATIVE DEVELOPMENT

Begin to differentiate colours. Differentiate marks on paper. Explore what happens when colours mix. Choose particular colours to use for a purpose. Work creatively on a small scale. Explore colour, texture, shape, form and space in two dimensions.

Key words

butterfly, wings, pattern

● Before the activity, photocopy Activity Sheet 10 – one per child.

● Show the children the butterfly on the Poster or in a book and invite them to talk about the shapes, patterns and colours on its wings.

● Help the children to notice that each side of the butterfly is the same.

● Using a mirror and a photograph of a butterfly. Show the children how to make half a butterfly into a whole one.

● Hand out copies of Activity Sheet 10 and a mirror per small group. Ask the children to colour in the finished half of the butterfly, and use mirrors to make a whole butterfly.

● Now ask them to colour in the other half, explaining that they should try to make both wings look exactly the same.

● End the lesson by playing the song 'Butterfly, butterfly'.

Questions

Is the music loud/soft/happy/sad?
How can we move to the music?

Extension

Help the children to make symmetrical butterfly shapes, by putting paint on to one side of a folded (and opened) piece of paper. Then refold it and open it again to show the pattern.

WORMS

Through close examination of real worms, the children will develop a natural curiosity about how they move, what size they can be and where they live. The activities will also develop their descriptive vocabulary and mathematical skills.

Wormwatch

RESOURCES

Per group, worm, clear container; ice cream tubs containing damp soil (in which to keep the worms); magnifying glasses

PHOTOCARD 6

KNOWLEDGE AND UNDERSTANDING OF THE WORLD

Show curiosity. Describe simple features of objects. Examine living things to find out more about them. **Find out about and identify some features of living things.**

Key words

big, fat, long, mouth, ring, short, thin, wiggle, worm, wriggle

SAFETY
● Before the activity, collect some worms of different sizes.

● Show the children Photocard 6.

● Divide the children into small groups, each of which has an adult supervisor. Give each group a magnifying glass and a worm and ask them to look at their worm.

● Point out the rings that encircle the worm at intervals.

● Encourage the children to describe and talk about the worms as they observe them – how they move, what they feel like.

● For those children who are happy to handle the worms, place a worm on their hand and ask what it feels like. Encourage them to look more closely at its skin, using a magnifying glass.

● Ensure that the children wash their hands after handling worms and soil.

Questions

What do worms look like?
How do worms move?
How do the worms feel?
Can you find the worm's head?
Does it have eyes, ears or a mouth?

Long worm, short worm

RESOURCES

Per pair, 2 counters; die; paper; wax crayons

Activity Sheet 11   **PHOTOCARD 6**

MATHEMATICAL DEVELOPMENT

Use language such as 'big' and 'little'. Begin to talk about shapes of objects. Order two or three items by length. Use language to describe the size of objects.

Key words

big, fat, long, short, thin

● Photocopy Activity Sheet 11 – one per pair.

● Show the children Photocard 6 and encourage them to talk about their findings from the Wormwatch activity.

● Talk about the different shapes and sizes of worms. Write the words 'long' and 'short' on the whiteboard.

● Ask the children to draw pictures of a long worm and a short worm and help them to write a caption for their pictures.

● Hand pairs of children a copy of Activity Sheet 11, a counter each and a die.

● Encourage them to play the worm 'snakes and ladders' game on the Activity Sheet with an adult.

Activity sheet 11

Questions

Did you see a long worm?
Did you see a short worm?
Did you see a thin worm?
Did you see a fat worm?
What other words describe the worms?

Squirmy earthworm

RESOURCES

COMMUNICATION, LANGUAGE AND LITERACY

Question why things happen and give explanations. Recognise rhythm in spoken words. Enjoy rhyming and rhythmic activities. Distinguish one sound from another. Use language for an increasing range of purposes. Enjoy listening to and using spoken language.

Key words

along, disappear, down, earthworm, ground, out, squirm, squirmy

● Remind the children of the worms they observed in the Wormwatch activity. Talk about how worms move in the ground.

● Play the poem 'Squirmy earthworm', and ask the children to listen to it carefully.

● Encourage the children to respond to the poem – to talk about how the poem describes the earthworm, what it does and where it lives.

● Play the poem again and ask the children to listen to the sounds of the words, such as 'wiggle' and 'squirm'. Ask them to talk about the words they like.

● Invite them to repeat the 'Squirmy earthworm' poem after you, and to move their hands to imitate the movement and direction of the worm in the ground.

Questions

Where does the earthworm live?
When does the earthworm wiggle out of the ground?
Why does the earthworm disappear into the ground? Where does it go?
Which words in the poem do you like? Why?

Magic growing pictures

RESOURCES

Per child, folded worm picture from Activity Sheet 12; pencils; crayons or felt-tip pens

PHYSICAL DEVELOPMENT

Engage in activities requiring hand-eye coordination. Use one-handed tools and equipment. Demonstrate increasing skill in control in the use of mark-making implements. Explore materials. Handle objects with increasing control.

Key words

draw, fold, longer, taller

● Photocopy Activity Sheet 12 – one per child. Cut out the strip with part of a worm on it and fold along the marks as shown.

● Give one to each child and show the children how to open out the folds of the paper. Next ask them to complete the missing section of the worm picture by drawing over the dotted lines.

● The children can colour in the picture using crayons, pencils or pens.

● Next show them how to fold the paper so that the middle section is no longer visible.

● Ask them to read with you the caption on the unopened paper ('a worm') and then to open it out and read the extended caption.

● You could also give the children the blank template to make other 'magic growing pictures' (to work either horizontally or vertically) of a bus/a longer bus, a snake/a longer snake, a car/a longer car, a ladder/a taller ladder, a flower/a taller flower, a tree/a taller tree and so on.

Questions

Where are the ends of the worm?
Where is the middle?
Which worm is longer/shorter?
Where will you start drawing the middle?

Look – no legs!

RESOURCES

Long sports mat

16

PHYSICAL DEVELOPMENT

Move spontaneously within an available space. Move freely with pleasure and confidence. Move in a range of ways, such as slithering, rolling. Go backwards and sideways as well as forwards. Experiment with different ways of moving. Move with confidence, imagination and safety.

Key words

forwards, backwards, sideways, creep, roll, slide, slither

How do minibeasts move? Encourage the children to think about and then imitate the way different minibeasts move, from wiggling and crawling to flying.

● During circle time, play the 'Playful pizzicato' track.

● Divide the children into small groups and challenge them to move like a minibeast from one end of a long mat to the other.

● Encourage the children to move in different directions – forwards, backwards, sideways.

● Remind them about the minibeasts they have observed that have no legs, such as worms or snails.

● Ask them to move like either a worm or a snail, and guess which one they are imitating.

● Invite the children to demonstrate their movements, and help the others to describe them using suitable vocabulary.

Questions
How can you move forwards/backwards/sideways? Can you move along the ground without using your feet? How does a worm move? How does a snail move?

What do minibeasts eat?

RESOURCES

Information books about minibeasts; paper; coloured crayons and pencils; scissors

PHOTOCARDS

17

KNOWLEDGE AND UNDERSTANDING OF THE WORLD

Show curiosity. Describe simple features of objects. Examine living things to find out more about them. Find out about and identify some features of living things.

Key words

animal, bird, eat, food, mole, people, soil

Talk to the children about what different minibeasts might like to eat. Encourage them to make suggestions based on the minibeasts they have learned about.

● Play the 'Worm song', while the children listen carefully. Repeat the track and encourage the children to join in.

● Talk about the song and discuss as a class who or what might eat worms (for example birds and moles).

● Show the children the minibeasts on the Photocards and Poster. Discuss what they eat. Look in books for more information about what minibeasts eat.

● Divide the children into small groups. Ask them to draw pictures of the food that minibeasts eat and the food that they don't eat.

● Write two large display labels – 'What minibeasts eat' and 'What minibeasts don't eat' – and encourage the children to cut out their pictures and stick them under the correct heading.

● Display your food chart next to the minibeast zoo (see pages 28-29).

Questions
Which animals eat worms? What do minibeasts eat? What don't they eat?

Ladybird, ladybird

RESOURCES

PHOTOCARD 7

18

Children enjoy familiar rhymes and this activity uses a well-known nursery rhyme to introduce and develop number skills.

● Show the children Photocard 7, or other books containing pictures of ladybirds, and ask them to name the insect.

● Invite them to describe its appearance.

● Ask the children if they know a nursery rhyme about a ladybird.

● Play 'Ladybird, ladybird' and encourage the children to listen carefully.

● Read the poem aloud a line at a time and help the children to make up actions for the second, third, fourth and last lines.

● Repeat the poem with the children doing the actions (for example, flapping their hands to show the ladybird flying) and joining in with the words if they can.

COMMUNICATION, LANGUAGE AND LITERACY

Listen to favourite nursery rhymes. Use talk to connect ideas and extend vocabulary. Listen to and join in with poems. Enjoy listening to and using spoken and written language. Make up songs, rhymes and poems.

Key words

black, crawl, feelers, ladybird, legs, red, spots, wings

Questions

What colour is the ladybird?
What colour are its spots?
How many spots does it have?
Does it have legs/wings? How many?

Extension

Encourage the children to make up their own 'Ladybird, ladybird' poem. Invite them to talk about what the ladybird could do, for example 'Fly to a leaf' or 'Fly to a flower'.

Ladybird spots

RESOURCES

Information books featuring ladybirds

PHOTOCARD 7

Activity Sheet 13

MATHEMATICAL DEVELOPMENT

Compare two groups of objects, saying when they have the same number. Use number names accurately. Find the total number of items in two groups by counting them. Count up to ten objects. Begin to count beyond ten. Use language such as 'more' or 'fewer'.

Key words

altogether, count, fewer, ladybird, more, same, spots

This activity also develops the children's understanding of numbers and their enjoyment of counting.

● Photocopy Activity Sheet 13 – one per child

● Show the children Photocard 7 and books containing pictures of ladybirds. Ask them if they all look the same.

● Help the children to count their spots. They may notice that some have two spots, others have seven or nine, and there are some with too many spots to count.

● Introduce the word 'same'. Show the children two identical items. Ask them if they are the same. Repeat this with pairs of items that are the same or different.

● Hand out Activity Sheet 13 and ask the children to look carefully at the pairs of ladybirds.

● Encourage them to draw spots on the spotless ladybird to match its partner.

Questions

Can you count the ladybird's spots?
Do they have the same number of spots?
Are these items the same? How?
How are they different?

Extension

Show the children pictures of two ladybirds and ask them to count the spots on each one. Ask them to count how many spots there are altogether.

A taste of honey

RESOURCES

Information books about bees; a jar of honey; a loaf of bread; safe knives; teaspoons; a large breadboard or other surface

PERSONAL, SOCIAL AND EMOTIONAL DEVELOPMENT

Show curiosity. Have a strong explanatory impulse. Explore within the environment. Be confident to try out new activities and speak in a group. Work as part of a group or class, taking turns and sharing fairly.

Key words

bee, bread, honey, honeycomb, knife, larva, spread

The children will be fascinated to learn more about the bees that produced the honey they get to taste in this activity.

● Show the children Photocard 8. Ask them to describe what they see.

● Point to the bees and explain that bees build honeycombs from wax, which they make inside their bodies.

● As a group, read a book about the life cycle of a bee. At the end, ask the children if they can think of a food that comes from bees.

● Show the children the jar of honey. Encourage them to discuss where it comes from and how it is made.

● Ask the children to wash their hands.

● Show the children how to take a spoonful of honey from the jar and then use a knife to spread it on a piece of bread.

● Invite the children to taste the honey. Ask them to describe how it tastes and to use the word 'sweet'. Encourage them to talk about other sweet foods.

Questions

Do you know where honey comes from?
What can you see in this picture?
Do you like the taste of honey?
What other sweet foods can you think of?

Honeycomb print

RESOURCES

Paper; trays of ready-mixed paint; honeycomb-shaped printing sponges; paint; brushes

CREATIVE DEVELOPMENT

Begin to differentiate colours. Work creatively on a small scale. Understand that different media can be combined. Choose particular colours to use for a purpose. Differentiate marks and movements on paper. Explore colour, texture, shape, form and space in two dimensions.

Key words

honeycomb, paint, print

This printing activity provides an opportunity for the children to explore ways of making marks and printing on paper, and to learn about bees.

● Show the children Photocard 8 and talk about the shape and colour of honeycomb.

● Demonstrate how to print honeycomb patterns by carefully dipping their sponges into the paint and placing the sponge on the paper.

● Tell the children you would like them to make some honeycomb prints. Help them to choose the colours they will use carefully.

● While the honeycomb prints dry, ask the children to paint a picture of a bee.

● When dry, the bees can be cut out and glued on to the honeycomb patterns.

Questions

What are the shapes on the honeycomb like?
What colour is the honeycomb?
What lives in it?
What colours can you see on a bee?

Buzzing bees

The children will enjoy 'The beehive song', and it will help to develop their counting skills.

● Before the session, make bee bodies from cotton wool dipped in yellow and black paint and cut out bee-shaped pieces of card.

● Start the activity by listening to 'The beehive song'. Tell the children that bees make honeycombs in a beehive and show them a picture of a beehive from an information book.

● Repeat the song and encourage the children to join in. You could hold up the correct number of fingers for the children to follow.

● Using drawing or painting materials, ask the children to help you paint or draw a big beehive for display.

● Help them to make bees by gluing the yellow and black cotton wool onto the cut out bee-shaped pieces of card.

● Glue the children's bees onto the beehive.

● Add wings, legs and feelers to the picture using felt-tip pens.

RESOURCES

Information book showing a beehive; small bee-shapes cut out of card; cotton wool; yellow and black paint; glue; black felt-tip pens

CREATIVE DEVELOPMENT

Join in favourite songs. Sing simple familiar songs. Begin to build a repertoire of songs. Sing simple songs from memory, recognise repeated sounds and match movements.

Key words
bees, buzz, hive, numbers one to five

Questions
Do you know what a beehive is?
What lives in a beehive?
How many bees live in the beehive in the song?
Can you show me one bee?
Can you show me two? (and so on up to five)

William the worm

RESOURCES

Scissors

COMMUNICATION, LANGUAGE AND LITERACY

Respond to simple instructions. Listen to stories with increasing attention and recall. Use language for an increasing range of purposes. Sustain attentive listening, responding to what has been heard by relevant comments, questions or actions.

Key words
worm, dog, woodlouse, snail, dragonfly, slug, bee, millipede, big, small, shell, feelers, wings, legs

Children will respond enthusiastically to this story-telling activity in which they practise putting the different parts of the story in to the correct order.

● Photocopy Activity Sheet 14 and hand out one per child.

● Show the children how to cut their sheet along the lines (giving help where needed) and lay the pictures out in front of them.

● Explain that the pictures tell a story and need to be put in the right order.

● Play the 'William the worm' story once, reminding the children to listen carefully.

● Play the track again, pausing after each section to give the children time to find the correct picture.

● When everyone has the pictures in the correct order, play 'William the worm' again, with the children following their pictures.

Questions
What sort of a creature is William?
Where is Sita the snail in your pictures?
Can you see Malcolm the millipede?
Does William find his family?

Extension
Give each child a piece of A4 paper. Ask them to colour in their 'William the worm' pictures and stick them onto a sheet of paper. Encourage the children to 'read' the story by following their pictures.

MINIBEAST MENAGERIE

This sequence of activities encourages children to recall and consider everything they have learnt about minibeasts as they make a large zoo and information book display.

Minibeast homes

RESOURCES

Cardboard boxes and jars with lids; paper bags; trays; bowls; buckets; card; string; pipe cleaners; soil; straw; sand; sawdust

KNOWLEDGE AND UNDERSTANDING OF THE WORLD

Investigate construction materials. Begin to try out a range of tools and techniques safely. Select tools and techniques. Construct with a purpose in mind. Build and construct with a range of objects.

Key words

minibeast names, soil, sand, straw, water, sawdust, safe, home

● Make some minibeast name labels and show them to the children one by one.

● Hold up the minibeast containers in turn and ask the children what sort of minibeast they could keep in it. Point out that the minibeast must not be able to escape and it must be kept healthy and safe.

● Ask a child to choose a container. Help him or her to choose the correct minibeast label to put on their container. For example, if the container is watertight, the label must be for a minibeast that lives in water. Attach the label.

● Show the children how the containers can be adapted to make safe and secure environments for each creature. For example, by piercing holes in a lid.

● Ask another child to choose a different container and repeat the activity.

Questions

What does the minibeast need?
Would it be able to live in this home?
How could we change the home to make it better for the minibeast?
Could the minibeast escape from this home?
How can we stop it?

Extension

Invite the children to talk about the animal homes they have made. What do they think is good about them? Is there anything they would like to change?

Create a zoo

RESOURCES

A flip chart/large sheet of paper or whiteboard; a large felt-tip pen; zoo leaflets or website printouts; construction and collage materials for the models (such as fabric, plasticine, pipe cleaners and wool); green and brown paper

PERSONAL, SOCIAL AND EMOTIONAL DEVELOPMENT

Have a positive approach to new experiences. Show willingness to tackle problems. Take initiatives and manage appropriate tasks. Be confident to try new activities, initiate ideas and speak in a group. Work as part of a group or class, taking turns and sharing fairly.

Key words

animal, minibeast, plan, zoo, cage

● Tell the children that you are going to make a minibeast zoo for the role-play corner.

● Ask the children if they have been to a zoo and encourage them to talk about how a minibeast zoo should be different from an ordinary zoo.

● Tell the children that they will not be able to keep real minibeasts in the zoo, so you are going to make models of minibeasts.

● In small groups, help the children to make minibeast models and cages using a variety of materials. Provide pictures of the creatures for them to look at whilst making their models.

● Ask the children what else they might need for their zoo. Write a list on the whiteboard. For example, containers, cages, signs, tickets to get in, money, a turnstile, a map, warning signs ('Do not touch' or 'Do not feed'), food for the minibeasts.

● Help the children to prepare minibeast habitats using foliage or green and brown paper. Remind them of the real habitats they have seen when collecting minibeasts.

● Arrange your minibeast zoo using the model minibeasts, cages and habitats.

Questions

Have you ever been to a zoo?
What did you see in the zoo?
What will we need for our minibeast zoo?

Extension

Encourage small groups to use the completed zoo for role-play. Ask the 'zoo-keepers' if they have cleaned out the cages and about feeding times. Ask the 'visitors' if they will come back, and which were their favourite animals.

Going to the zoo

RESOURCES

Information books about minibeasts

21   PHOTOCARDS

CREATIVE DEVELOPMENT

Join in favourite songs. Tap out simple repeated rhythms. Begin to build up a repertoire of songs. Sing to themselves and make up simple songs. Sing simple songs from memory.

Key words

too, zoo

● Play the song 'Going to the zoo'. Encourage the children to join in the chorus.

● Ask the children which animals were in the song. Ask them which animal had 'a long trunk swinging' and 'great big ears', which animals were 'scritch, scritch scratching' and 'hanging by their long tails' and which was 'all huff huff a-puffing'.

● Help the children to make up some of their own words, substituting minibeasts for the large animals.

● Hold up a picture of a minibeast on a Photocard or in a book and ask the children to suggest some words for what it might do, giving the prompts – for example, (spider) 'spin spin spinning', (worm) 'wig wig wiggling', (snail) 'slime slime sliming'.

● Write these words on the whiteboard or make labels for them and ask the children to think of other minibeast words.

● Sing the children's song to the same tune and with the same chorus.

Minibeasts big book

RESOURCES

Large sheets of card and paper; a long-arm stapler; pencils; felt-tip pens; coloured pencils; (large) information books about minibeasts; glue

COMMUNICATION, LANGUAGE AND LITERACY

Use vocabulary focused on subjects that are important to them. Build up vocabulary that reflects the breadth of their experiences. Extend vocabulary especially by grouping and naming. Extend their vocabulary exploring the meanings of new words.

Key words

eyes, feelers, legs, wings, short, long, round

● Begin by showing the group a big book and pointing out features, such as cover and title.

● Ensure that the words for the body parts of the minibeasts are visible somewhere in the classroom – on the board or as labels.

● Help the children to choose a minibeast that they can draw and label.

● Point out its features – the number of legs it has, its feelers, eyes and wings and encourage them to notice the shape of the minibeast's body.

● They could draw the minibeast in its habitat – for example, under a stone, on a leaf, in the soil, on a flower.

● Using an information book, help them to write labels for their picture.

● Ask the children to glue each of their minibeast pictures onto large pieces of card. Work together to put the minibeasts cards in alphabetical order.

● Staple the pieces together to make a big book and display it in the minibeast zoo area.

Questions

Does the minibeast have legs/wings/feelers? How many? What is its body like? What letter does its name begin with?

Display ideas

Displays can be used to stimulate interest in a topic or to reinforce an idea or skill. Displaying children's work can add value to what they have done, raise self-esteem and help them learn to share. Good displays can lead to a stimulating environment and give great pleasure, both to the children who create the displays and their parents and carers who come to admire them. The following display suggestions make use of the activities and resources in this pack.

Display tips

● Wallpapers make long-lasting backgrounds that do not fade as quickly as sugar papers.
● Corrugated card helps to provide 3-D parts to flat displays. It is particularly useful for trees and logs.
● Borders around displays help to focus eyes on the display contents.
● Ceilings, cupboards and windows are valuable display areas.

Minibeast alphabet frieze

● Use a long display board in a corridor or hall, or around two walls of a classroom.

● Fix 26 pieces of A4 card to the display board, lettered Aa to Zz, and arrange them in a long line at child height.

● Ask the children to draw, or cut out from magazines or leaflets, pictures of minibeasts. Ask them to say the name of the minibeast, to listen to the first sound and to decide on which card it belongs. They should check with an adult before gluing the pictures on to the cards.

● Ask them for which letters there are the most minibeasts and for which there are the fewest.

  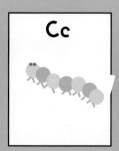 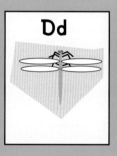 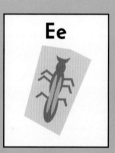 

Where do I live? (see page 13)

● With the children, make a large display-sized picture of a minibeast environment. Use light brown paper with painted or printed outlines of tree trunks, flowers, grass, stones, twigs and so on. Make sure it has an 'underground' area for worms.

● Draw and cut out some outlines of items, such as stones and leaves, and fix these on to the picture with sticky tape on one edge. This allows them to be lifted so that minibeasts can be placed underneath them.

● Help the children to cut out and colour in the minibeast pictures from Activity Sheet 4 and to stick them in the appropriate place on the minibeast environment display. (Attach a label to each minibeast.)

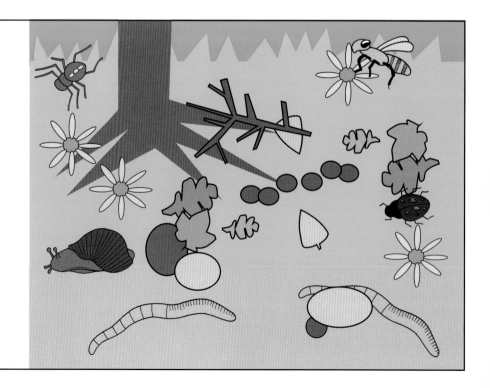

The ants go marching (see page 12)

● Cover a display board with red paper. Make a border by drawing (or printing from clip art) a series of black musical notes on a white background and then photocopying it for repeats.

● Write the title of the song 'The ants go marching' using cut-out letter-templates in black.

● On separate strips of paper, write the first line of each verse. Illustrate it with a row of larger-than-life ants drawn and cut out by the children. If you do not have enough ants (you need a total of fifty-five), make colour copies of some of the children's pictures.

● Involve the children, according to their ability, in counting the ants for each line.

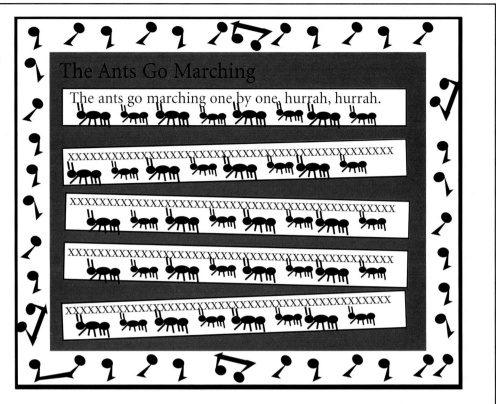

How many legs? (see page 15)

● On a display board at child height, arrange seven pieces of different-coloured A3 paper in a horizontal line. Make a border using white paper and add printed black animal footprints (all going in the same direction around the border).

● Write the following numbers and words in order at the tops of the pieces of paper:
● No legs
● Two legs
● Three legs
● Four legs
● Six legs
● Eight legs
● Too many legs to count

● Along the bottom of each piece of paper, put the appropriate number of spots for the number at the top of the page (no spots on the first piece, two on the second and so on).

● Help the children to draw or cut out pictures of minibeasts and animals. Ask them to count the legs and to use information books, CD-ROMs or pictures to check that they have drawn the right number on their own pictures.

● Show them how to pin their minibeasts and animals on to the correct paper.

● Discuss with the children which pieces of paper have no creatures on them, and why. Can they find a minibeast with two or four legs?

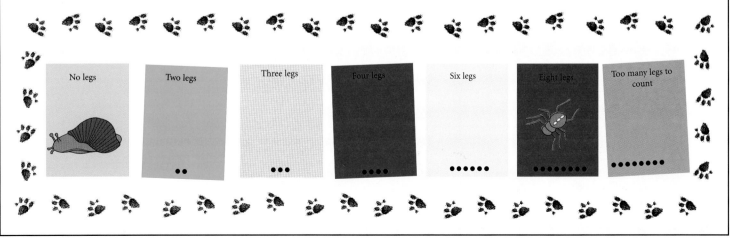

Working with parents and carers

Each time you begin a new topic with the children, remember to pass this information to their parents or carers. You can do this by putting a notice on the parent and carer board, telling them what the current topic is. Alternatively, you can send a letter home to explain which themes will be covered. The letter can give parents and carers ideas for activities they can do at home, both to extend their child's learning and to help the child make connections between home and the classroom.

You might want to use the letter below as a template:

Dear parents,

Our topic from ………………….. to ……………………….
is Minibeasts. This topic helps the children to learn about the small animals in our surroundings (the ones that fit into a matchbox). We would appreciate it if you would collect matchboxes which the children will use for comparing the size of things.

Do please come and see the exciting displays of work that the children will be helping to make.

Yours sincerely,

On the next page, we have provided some simple activities that can be carried out at home to support the children's understanding of the 'Minibeasts' topic. Each one is designed to be done after the school activities have been completed, and uses items easily found around the house. You may want to photocopy the page, and add dates to show when you will cover the activity in class, before sending it home.

Parents and carers may wish to ask questions or make comments about the activities that they have tried at home. Such discussion will make them feel more involved in their child's development and more willing to continue the 'at-home' activities.

We shall be covering the following activities over the next few weeks as part of the topic 'Minibeasts'. You may wish to try some of the related activities once we have covered the main activity in class in order to reinforce your child's learning.

MINIBEASTS ACTIVITY IDEAS

Activity: What have we found? _____
- Look for minibeasts in the garden, or whilst out on a walk with your child.
- Encourage him or her to guess the name of the minibeast and talk about its appearance.

Activity: Guess who? _____
- Play 'Minibeast I Spy' using minibeast books from the library or any you have at home.
- Choose a minibeast from a set of pictures and say 'I spy with my little eye a minibeast beginning with…'
- Encourage your child to ask questions to help him or her guess. For example 'How many legs does it have?'

Activity: Web words _____
- Help your child to think of other words beginning, like 'web', with the sound 'w'.
- Encourage him or her to think of words beginning with other sounds; for example the first letter of their name or a brother or sister's name, or 'Mum' or 'Dad'.
- Ask him or her to draw pictures of three or four things beginning with the same letter sound.

Activity: Dragonfly _____
- Make some dragonfly wings with your child.
- Cut large wing shapes out of card and decorate with coloured paints and paper glitter and ribbons.
- Use safety pins to attach these to your child's back. Encourage him or her to move around like a dragonfly.

Activity: Spirals _____
- Look for snails in the garden or out on a walk, or look at pictures in books.
- Talk about the pattern of a snail's shell and make a spiral collage using coloured wool, ribbon and string.

Activity: Caterpillar
- Look for caterpillars in the garden or out on a walk.
- Encourage your child to notice and talk about their colours, and afterwards draw a picture of a caterpillar.

Activity: Long or short? _____
- Using modelling dough, make worms of different lengths and thicknesses with your child.
- Encourage him or her to use appropriate words – 'long', 'short', 'fat' and 'thin' – to describe their worms.

Activity: Ladybird, ladybird _____
- Talk about the colour of ladybirds – red with black spots.
- Encourage your child to look for red objects and black objects at home and when out on a trip.
- How many can he or she count?

Activity: A taste of honey _____
- Taste honey with your child. Encourage him or her to talk about and taste other sweet foods.
- Which is his or her favourite sweet food? Sweets, biscuits or fruit such as bananas and raisins. Why?

Activity: Minibeast menagerie _____
- Look through old magazines and greetings cards to find pictures of minibeasts.
- Together make a book of minibeast pictures.
- Enjoy telling stories about the pictures.

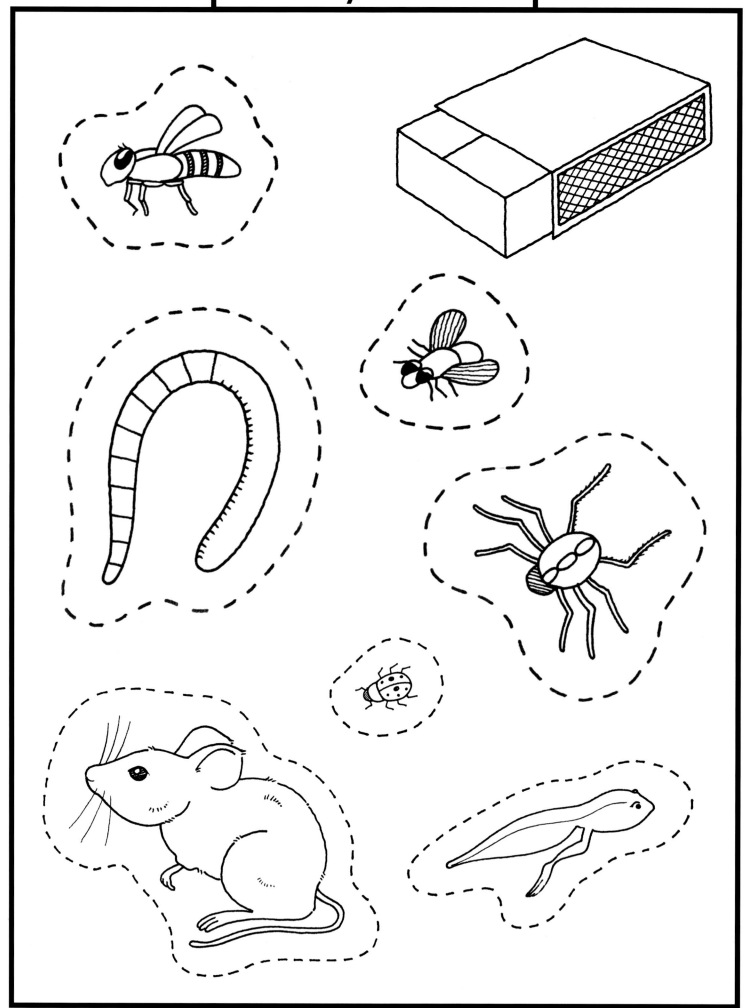

Foundations   **Minibeasts**   A & C Black

I am a worm
I have 0 legs

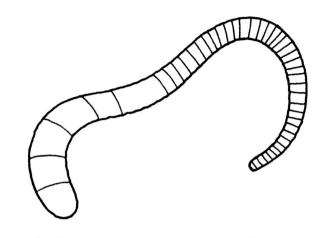

I am a bee
I have 6 legs

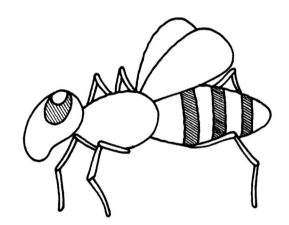

I am a snail
I have 0 legs

I am an ant
I have 6 legs

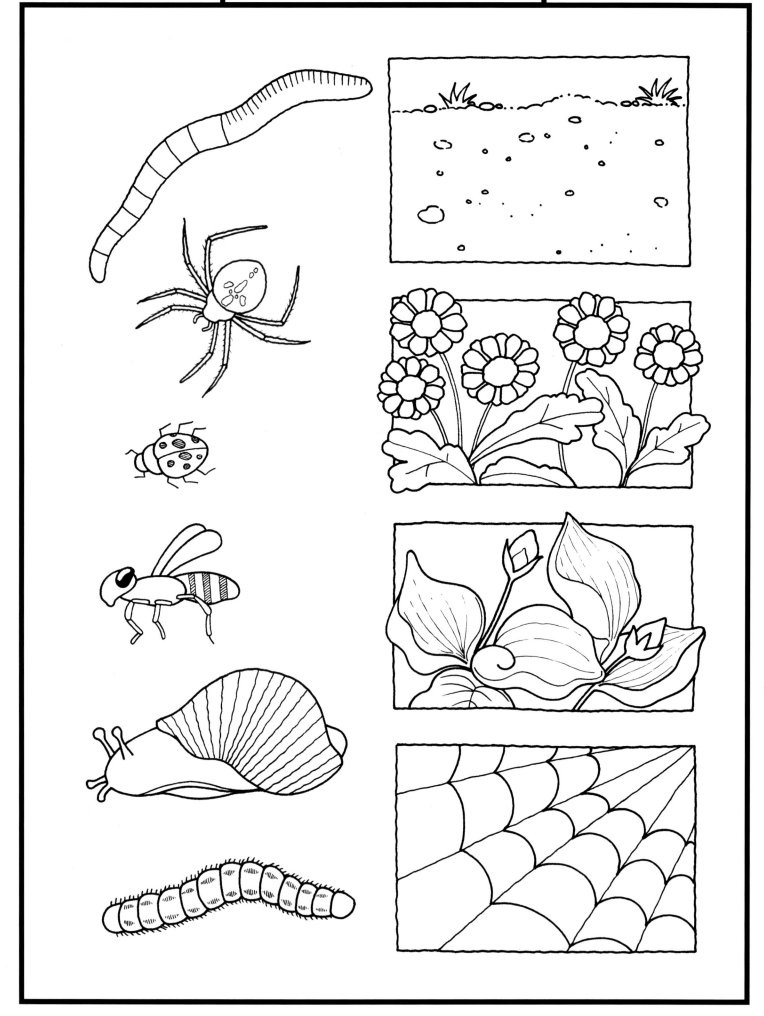

Foundations   **Minibeasts**   A & C Black

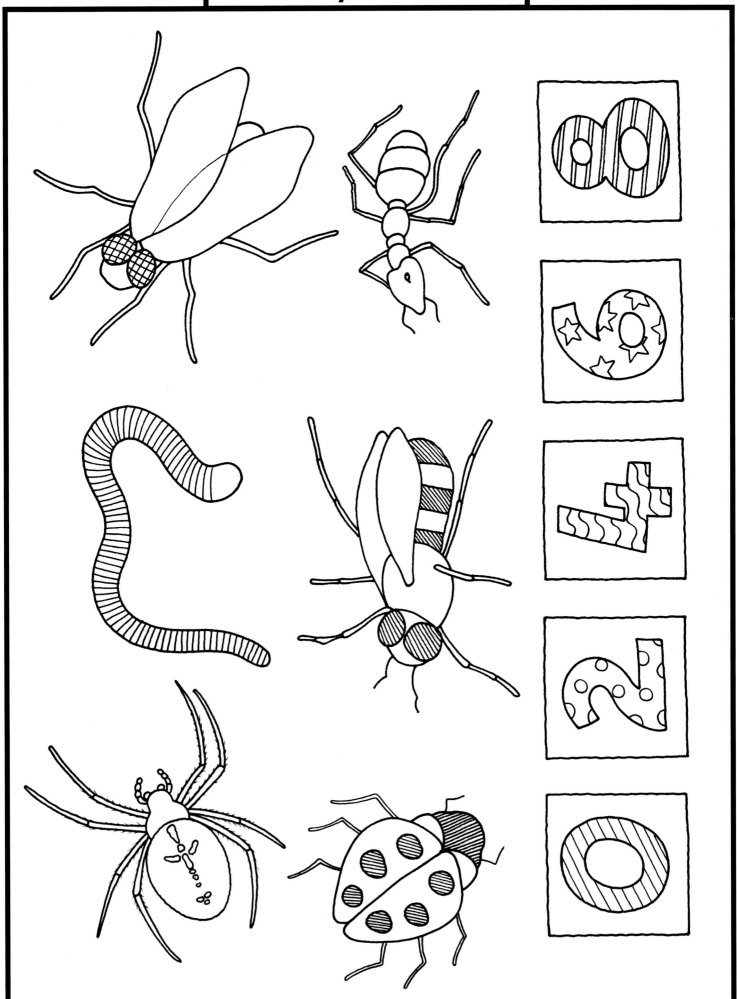

Foundations   **Minibeasts**   A & C Black

Activity sheet 6

Foundations   **Minibeasts**   A & C Black

Activity sheet 8

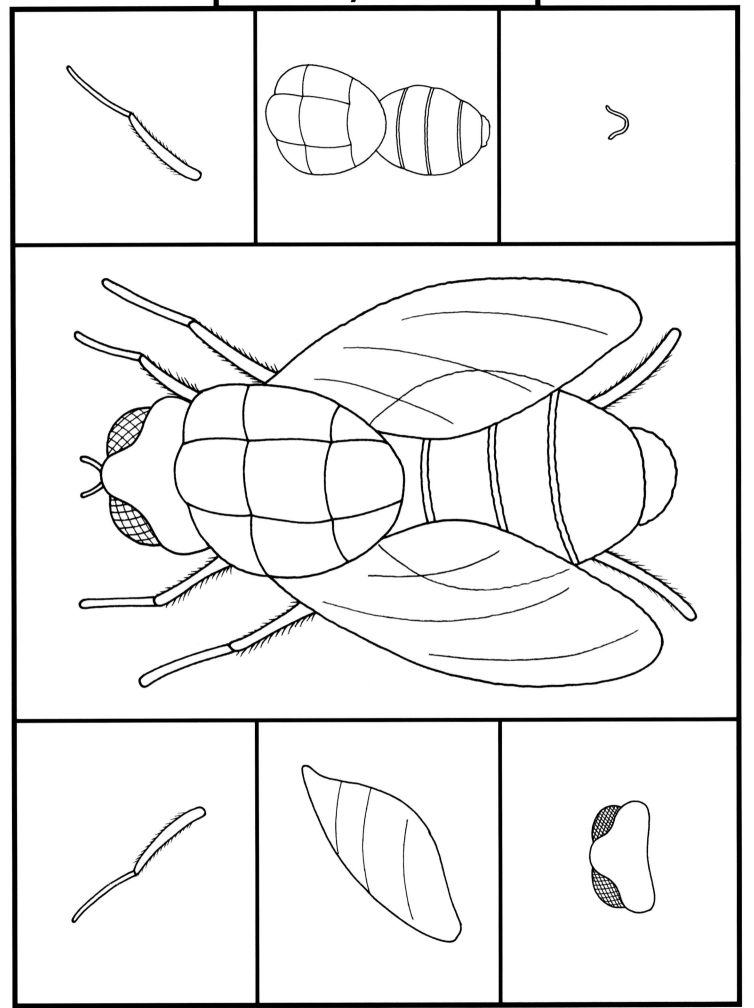

Foundations   **Minibeasts**   A & C Black

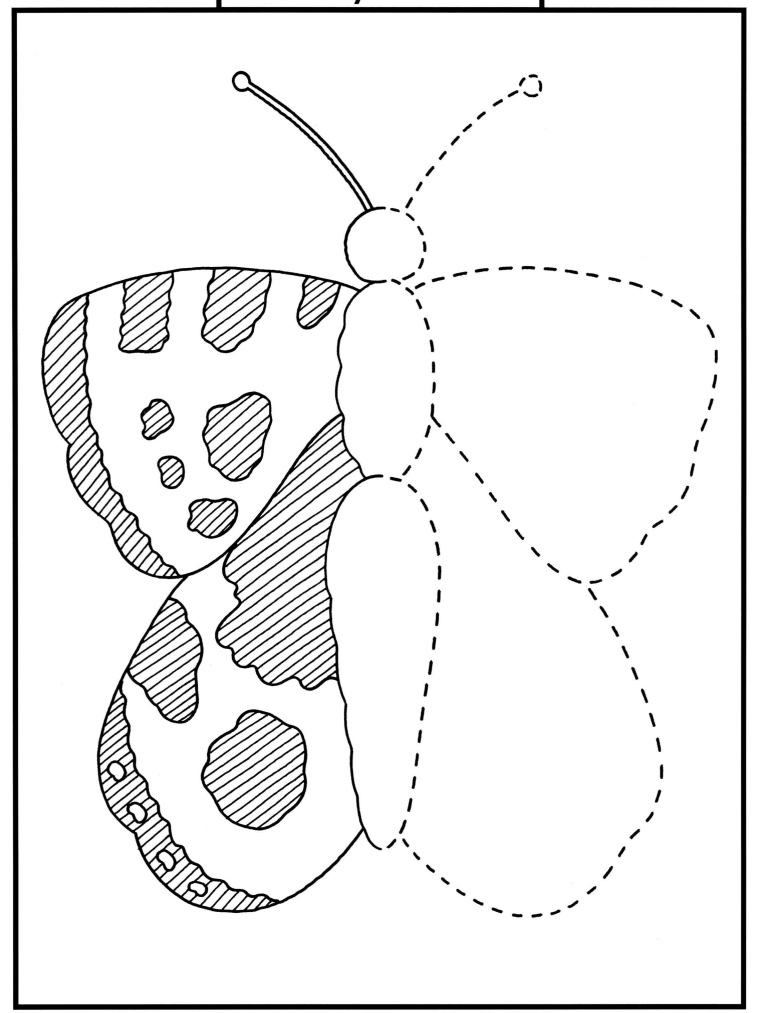

Activity sheet 11

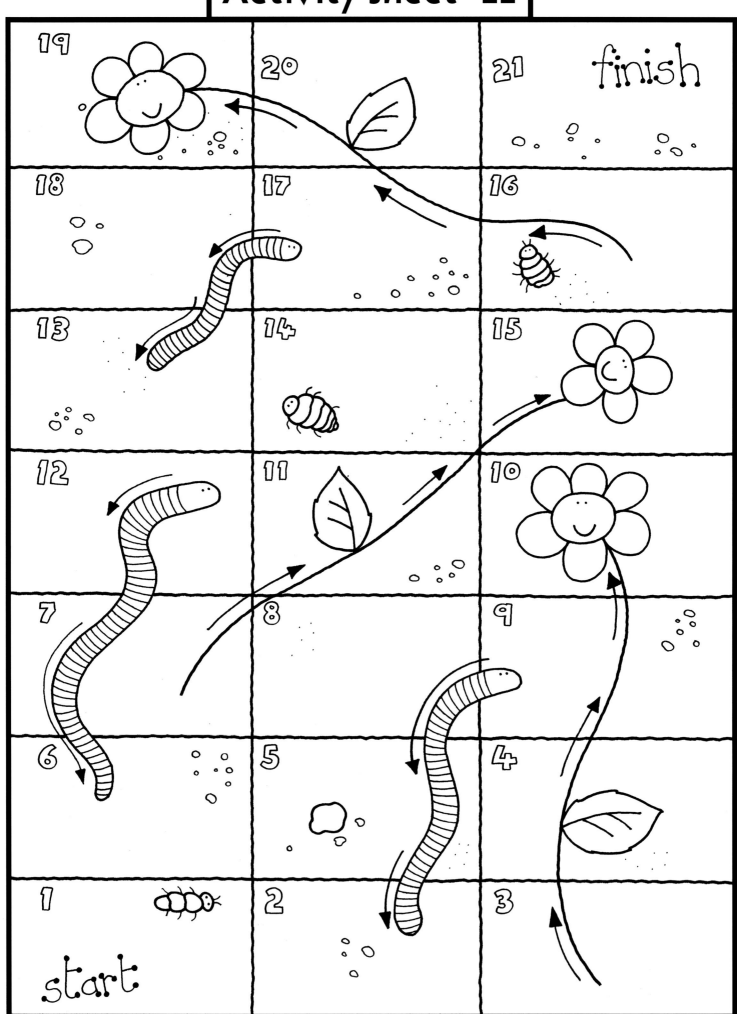

Activity sheet 12

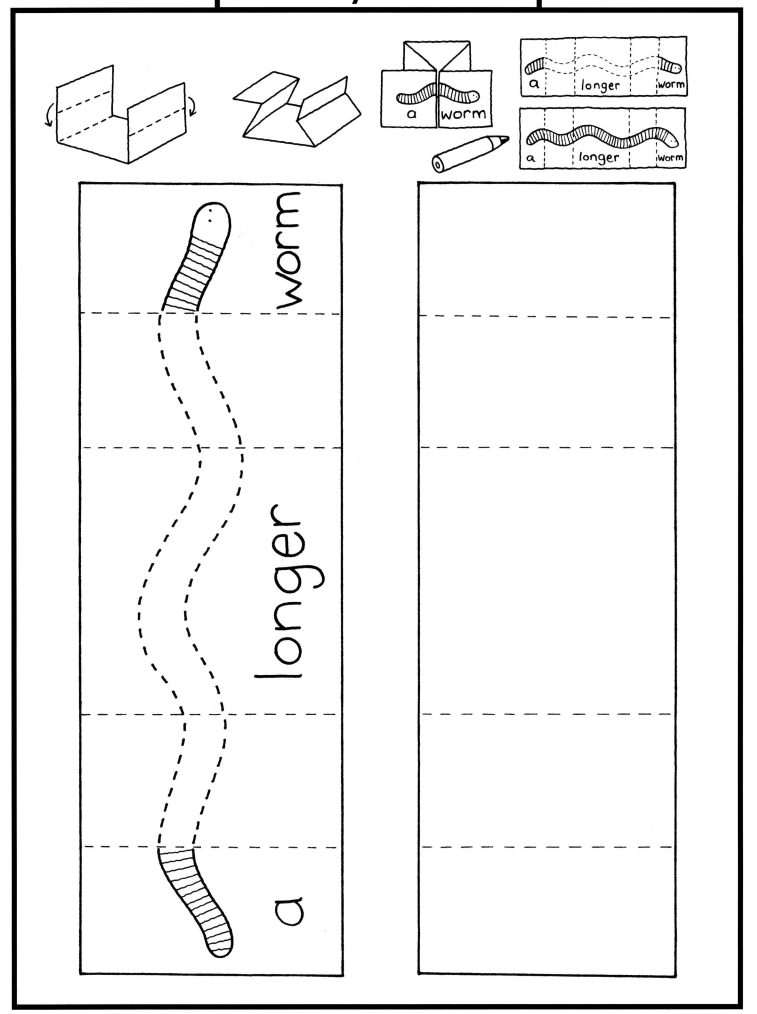

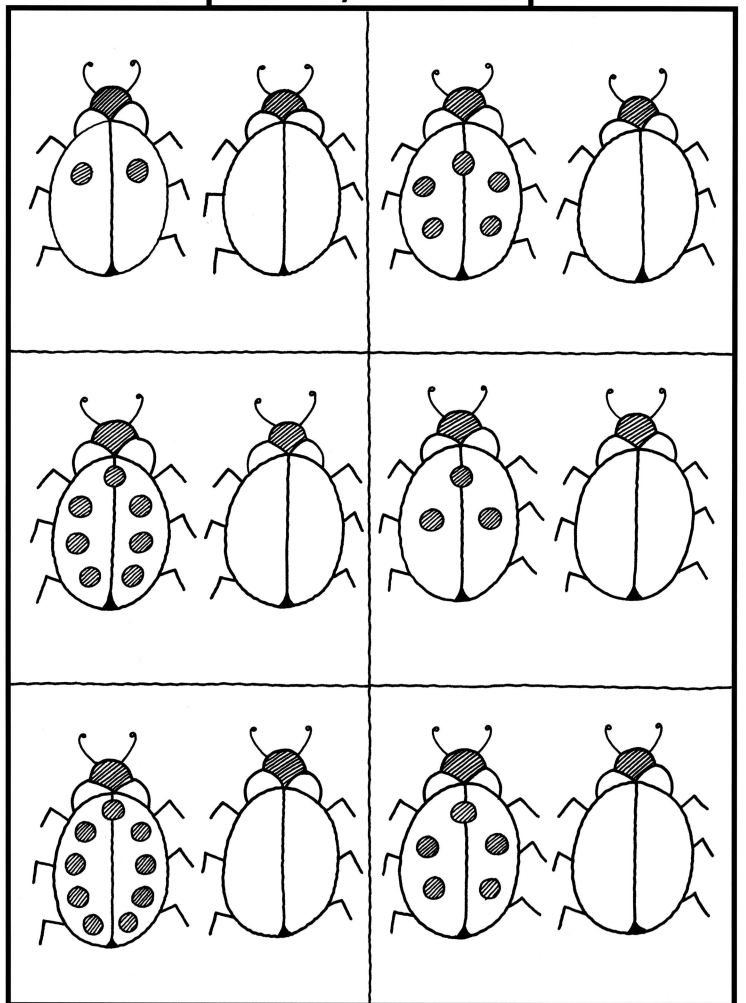

Foundations   Minibeasts   A & C Black

Activity sheet 14

Index

Resources list

This is a list of all of the materials needed to carry out the activities in this pack.

Writing/drawing/painting materials

- Coloured wax crayons
- Coloured pencils
- Ready-mixed paints in a range of colours
- Washable felt-tip pens
- Chalks
- Paint brushes
- Water pots
- Printing sponges

Papers (in a range of colours)

- Sugar paper
- Tissue paper
- Card
- Cartridge paper
- Newspaper
- Wallpaper
- Shiny/glossy paper

Craft/modelling/construction materials

- Safety scissors
- Long arm stapler
- Glue and glue brushes
- Sticky tape/double-sided sticky tape
- Masking tape
- Coloured modelling dough
- Coloured acetate/cellophane
- Fabric scraps in a variety of colours and patterns
- Coloured wool scraps
- Glitter
- Plastic tubs and pots
- Cardboard tubes
- String
- Coloured and shiny threads/ribbons
- Cardboard boxes in different sizes
- Pipe cleaners
- Cotton wool

Resources for investigative work

- Containers/tools for collecting minibeasts
- Transparent containers for keeping minibeasts
- All habitats for minibeasts should contain material from the environment in which they were found. Also provide food if the minibeasts are being kept inside for a period of time.
- Snail food (10 parts oatmeal, 1 part calcium carbonate (available from pharmacies), mix with water to form paste)
- Magnifying containers
- Perspex sheets
- Plastic magnifiers
- Plastic mirrors
- Play slime (500g cornflour, 300ml water, food dye)
- Large bowls
- Plastic sieves/griddles

Other resources

- Matchboxes
- Honey
- Mini car brochures
- Bread/Breadboard
- Counters/dice
- Long sports mat
- Flipchart/whiteboard
- Pictures of miniskirts/minibuses
- Information books about large range of minibeasts
- Paper bags
- Teaspoons
- Minibeast CD-Roms
- Minibeast pictures
- Safety knives
- Large cubes